Binary Trees Unleashed

An In-Depth Study of Tree Structures

Table of Contents

Chapter 1. Introduction

In this Special Report, "Binary Trees Unleashed: An In-Depth Study of Tree Structures", we unravel the intrinsic complexities and explore the profound characteristics of binary trees, a fundamental concept of data structures prominently used in Computer Science. Being a highly technical subject, we aim to lay it down in a comprehensible and grounded manner, intended to enrich both the seasoned programmer who seeks a deeper understanding and the amateur programmer who aspires to delve into the mesmerizing world of data structures. By dissecting these seemingly complicated systems and presenting their operations in an accessible light, this report offers a solid foundation in binary trees and a stepping stone to the broader field of non-linear data structures. This invaluable knowledge could indeed serve as your gateway to a more advanced level of programming. Buckle up for an intellectual journey—fair warning—it may unleash a new perspective on problem-solving through computational thinking.

Chapter 2. Introduction to Binary Trees

Binary trees are a fundamental data structure in Computer Science, widely used in a multitude of contexts due to their structured nature and valuable application potential. Providing an efficient means to store and organize data, binary trees find their practical use in everyday scenarios, from visual scene rendering in games to lookup operations in databases.

Before diving into the technical aspects, it's important to comprehend what binary trees are fundamentally. The term 'binary tree' is unambiguously self-explanatory. In essence, binary trees are tree-like structures encompassing nodes, with each node containing at most two children, thereby rendering the term 'binary'. These two node children are distinguished as left child and right child.

2.1. Structure of Binary Trees

Every binary tree consists of nodes, and these nodes are structured in a hierarchical fashion. The topmost node of the binary tree is typically referred to as the 'root node'. A node that adds another node under it is known as its 'parent', while the node that is under another node is its 'child'.

Each node encompasses the following components:

- **Key**: An attribute with a specific value that identifies the node.

- **Left Child**: Pointer to the left child node.

- **Right Child**: Pointer to the right child node.

- **Parent**: Pointer to the parent node (not compulsory but sometimes useful).

The root node is the only node in the tree that doesn't have a parent. If a node doesn't bear any children, it is referred to as a 'leaf' or a 'terminal' node. The height of a binary tree is the maximum number of edges between the root node and the farthest leaf node. Conversely, the depth or level of a node is determined by the number of edges traversed from the root to that particular node.

The visual representation of a binary tree will solidify your basic understanding:

```
     (Root)
        |
    ---------------
    |             |
(Left Child) (Right Child)
```

2.2. Types of Binary Trees

Binary trees can be classified into several types, each exhibiting unique properties and fulfilling specific requirements. These types have been listed below:

1. **Full Binary Tree**: A binary tree in which every node has two children except the leaf nodes.

2. **Complete Binary Tree**: A binary tree in which all levels except possibly the last are completely filled, and all nodes are as left as possible.

3. **Perfect Binary Tree**: A binary tree that is both full and complete. All leaf nodes will be at the same level, and this level has maximum number of nodes.

4. **Balanced Binary Tree**: A binary tree where the difference between the heights of left and right subtrees for every node is not more than k (mostly 1).

5. **Degenerate (or pathological) Binary Tree**: A binary tree where each parent node has only one associated child node. This is essentially equivalent to a linked list.

2.3. Binary Tree Traversals

Visiting every node in the binary tree is called a 'traversal'. This is crucial in understanding and implementing tree-based algorithms. There are mainly three types of traversals in a binary tree, which are defined based on the order in which nodes are visited:

1. **Preorder Traversal** (Root – Left Child – Right Child)

2. **Inorder Traversal** (Left Child – Root – Right Child)

3. **Postorder Traversal** (Left Child – Right Child – Root)

Each of these traversal methods showcases its own set of advantages and perfectly suits certain operations. It is vital to choose an appropriate traversal method based on the task at hand.

2.4. Applications of Binary Trees

Binary trees, due to their structured nature and valuable properties, have extensive applications and are used in various domains. Some of the main applications of binary trees are:

1. Binary trees form the basis of many efficient non-linear data structures such as Binary Search Trees (BST), AVL Trees, Heap Trees, and others.

2. Binary Space Partitioning (BSP) trees, a variant of binary trees, are used in computer graphics to render scenes.

3. Used in searching algorithms, where binary trees significantly reduce the time complexity.

4. Used in compression algorithms such as Huffman coding, which

leverages binary trees for its implementation.

5. Many databases use binary trees and their variants like B-Tree and T-Tree to store data in a structured and quickly retrievable manner.

Binary trees, due to their hierarchical structure, are a vital part of Computer Science, aiding the design of efficient algorithms and dynamic processes. They not only add structure to data but also make it possible to implement complex tasks efficiently. Reflecting on the core aspects, grasp of binary trees provides a springboard to further delve into more intricate data structures thereby intensifying your problem-solving abilities. However, this is just the surface of binary trees. As you delve deeper, you will encounter larger complexities and a world of intriguing concepts waiting to be discovered.

Chapter 3. Underlying Principles and Terminology

Mathematically, binary trees are hierarchically structured stratified trees where each node can attach to a maximum of two nodes. Although seemingly simplistic, this humble yet efficient model has been able to solve numerous complex problems in data formatting and data management. From search algorithms to queue operations, binary trees have come to be acknowledged as one of the cornerstones of computation.

3.1. Foundations of a Binary Tree

The inception of a binary tree starts from the conventionally called 'root'. The root is the paterfamilias or the 'origin node' in the tree. Each node in the tree possesses a data element, and references/pointers connecting to two other distinct nodes. The universally followed nomenclature, derived from botanical analogy, christens the two nodes as 'left child' and 'right child'.

It's pertinent to understand that each node is potentially the root of its subset binary tree. Therefore, a node's "left" or "right" child could further branch into their subsequent "left" or "right" children, thus continuing the tree growth.

```
        Root
       /    \
     Left   Right
     / \    / \
  Left Right Left Right
```

3.2. Tree Vocabularies

As with any specialized field, understanding the underlying binary trees requires familiarization with certain terminologies.

- **Parent Node**: A node, which has nodes growing out of it, is their parent node. For instance, in the depicted tree, the root is the parent of the "left child" and "right child."

- **Child Node**: A node is considered a child node if it sprouts from another node. In the referred example, both "left" and "right" nodes are children to the root.

- **Sibling Nodes**: Nodes that stem from the same parent node are regarded as siblings.

- **Leaf Node**: The terminal nodes, or those without any children, are known as leaves or leaf nodes.

The unidirectional feature in most binary tree structures results in terms like 'ancestor' and 'descendant'. The ancestor node is a node that exists on the path from the root to the said node. Conversely, a descendant is a node that exists on the path from a node to any of its leaves.

When we reference the 'height' of a binary tree, we're talking about the length of the longest path from the root to a leaf. The 'depth' of a node, on the other hand, pertains to the length of the path from the root to that particular node. The 'level' is defined as the collection of all nodes at the same depth. The root is conventionally at level '0'.

3.3. Binary Tree Properties

Like other stratified structures, binary trees come up with a set of properties that ascertain their performance and behavior. The count of total nodes 'n' on any 'l' level is a maximum of 2^l. Also, a binary tree with 'h' height has a maximum of $2^h - 1$ nodes. It is important to comprehend that these properties hold up for complete binary trees where all levels except possibly the last are completely filled, and the nodes are as far left as possible.

Another significant term is a 'Balanced Binary Tree', which maintains a difference in heights of left and right subtrees of every node not more than 1. Such trees provide the benefit of efficient searching and operation complexity.

3.4. Classification of Binary Trees

Depending on node formation and characteristics, binary trees are classified into types: Binary Search Tree (BST), AVL tree, Red-Black, and B-trees, to name a few.

- **Binary Search Trees**: In BST, for each node, all elements in the left subtree are less, and in the right subtree are more than the node. This arrangement simplifies the search operation.

- **AVL Trees**: Named after inventors Adelson-Velsky and Landis, AVL trees are self-balancing Binary Search Trees that maintain their height balancing property after every insertion or deletion, thus ensuring efficient data management.

- **Red-Black Trees**: Similar to AVL Trees, Red-Black Trees also self-balance; however, they follow another property: each node is assigned one extra bit for denoting its color (red or black), which aids in maintaining balance after operations.

- **B-Trees**: Primarily used in databases and filesystems, B-trees are a generalization of binary search trees that allows for a variable number of child nodes.

Understanding the fundamental principles and technical nomenclature is key to unraveling the potential binary trees bring to the data structure landscape. With this knowledge, the exploration of their applications and in-depth operations becomes a more attainable goal. Their significance is deeply embedded in computer science, often providing smart solutions to intricate problems. Picking the right kind of binary tree for a specific application can drastically influence the performance of the operations.

Upcoming chapters will dive into further details of these types of trees, their operations, algorithms, and virtually potential applications that showcase how integral binary trees are to modern computing.

Chapter 4. Types of Binary Trees

Binary trees are a fundamental part of computer science and serve as the underlying structure for many applications. A binary tree is defined as a tree where any given node can have either no, one, or two child nodes. While there are many possible configurations or types of binary trees, the most typically studied varieties are the full binary tree, the complete binary tree, and the perfect binary tree. We will dive into these topics one by one, articulating their unique definitions, properties, and applications.

4.1. Full Binary Tree

A full binary tree, also known as a proper binary tree, is characterized by a tree in which every node has either 0 or 2 children. In other words, no node in a full binary tree has exactly one child node. This attribute leads to some key structural properties in the tree as a whole.

Every full binary tree has an even number of leaf nodes (nodes with no children). This comes from the property that nodes can only have either 0 or 2 child nodes. We can derive this fact mathematically with the formula; if L represents leaf nodes and I the internal nodes, then in any full binary tree, $L = I + 1$.

This type of tree is extremely prevalent in applications where binary decisions are made. For example, full binary trees are used in creating binary decision diagrams (used in optimization algorithms) and Huffman coding trees used to compress data.

4.2. Complete Binary Tree

Another noteworthy type of binary tree is the complete binary tree. In a complete binary tree, every level of the tree is fully filled with nodes except possibly for the last level, which is filled from the left side.

Complete binary trees are known for their efficiency in element access and manipulation. They are commonly used in binary heaps, which serve as a basis for Heap Sort, one of the most efficient sorting algorithms. This type of tree can be easily represented using an array structure which makes it extremely memory efficient. A node with an index i has its left child at the index 2*i + 1 and its right child at 2*i + 2 with i starting from 0.

A significant property is that for a complete binary tree with n nodes, the height of the tree is log(n+1). This makes operations like insertion, deletion and searching quite efficient (O(log n)).

4.3. Perfect Binary Tree

A perfect binary tree is perhaps the most balanced form of a binary tree. In this configuration, all the internal nodes have two children and all leaf nodes are at the same level or same depth. This means every level of the tree (including the last level) is fully filled.

A perfect binary tree with a height h has 2^(h+1) - 1 nodes in total, which means it possesses the maximum number of nodes for a given height compared to any other binary tree configuration. For instance, if the number of nodes is n, then the height of a perfect binary tree is log(n+1) - 1.

The perfect binary tree is applied in many algorithmic solutions for its property of keeping the tree balanced. It is used in Tries for keeping the dictionary in order, in AVL Trees for preserving the balance factor and in B-trees used in databases for disk reads.

4.4. Skewed Binary Tree

Skewed binary trees, meanwhile, have a configuration where every node has only one child, except for the leaf nodes. They can be further divided into two types: left-skewed and right-skewed.

In a left-skewed binary tree, every node has only a left child whereas in a right-skewed binary tree, every node has only a right child. A skewed binary tree with n nodes has a tree height of n, meaning that its operations have a time complexity of $O(n)$, which can result in significant inefficiencies.

4.5. Balanced Binary Tree

A balanced binary tree is one in which the left and right subtrees of every node differ in height by no more than one. This property aids in ensuring that operations performed on the tree (like insertion, deletion, and access) have relatively similar and predictable times, regardless of the values used.

One common use of balanced binary trees is in the AVL tree (named after inventors Adelson-Velsky and Landis), a self-balancing binary search tree. The AVL tree adjusts itself during insert and delete operations to maintain its balanced property.

While there are details beyond what's been captured here, the types of binary trees discussed above provide a comprehensive overview and serve as the foundational concepts in understanding binary trees and their applications. Each has its own unique set of properties, uses, and reasons why they might be chosen in a particular situation over another. They each embody the beauty and complexity of data structures present in computer science and certainly serve to elaborate on how we can use binary trees to solve a multitude of problems.

Chapter 5. Tree Traversal Strategies: Preorder, Inorder, and Postorder

Before we delve into the different strategies for tree traversal, it's imperative to understand what traversal means. Traversal, in the context of trees, refers to the process of visiting each node in a tree structure exactly once in a specific order. This order can differ based on the traversal strategy being utilized—namely Preorder, Inorder, or Postorder.

Traversing a tree is a key operation as it allows for every element in the tree to be processed. The processing could be of several types, such as searching for a node, printing the content of a node, or any other operation that needs to be executed on each node. This traversal is accomplished by utilizing recursive algorithms that make the traversal process systematic and efficient.

5.1. Preorder Traversal (Root, Left, Right)

In the Preorder traversal method, we visit the root node first, then traverse the left subtree, and finally the right subtree.

This process can be implemented through a recursive algorithm where we first process the root node, followed by recursive calls for the left subtree and then the right subtree. If the tree is empty, we simply return without performing any operations.

The Preorder traversal is primarily used for copying a tree as it maintains the original structure of the tree. It can also be used to obtain prefix notation (also known as Polish notation) of an expression tree.

Here is a simple algorithm to achieve Preorder traversal:

```
1. Visit the root.
2. Traverse the left subtree, i.e., call Preorder(left-
subtree)
3. Traverse the right subtree, i.e., call
Preorder(right-subtree)
```

5.2. Inorder Traversal (Left, Root, Right)

In Inorder traversal, the left subtree is traversed first, then the root node is visited, and finally, the traversal moves to the right subtree.

This traversal strategy is prominently used in binary search trees where the Inorder traversal retrieves data in sorted order. In an expression tree, this traversal can help obtain the infix notation representing the expression.

Here is the algorithm to achieve Inorder traversal:

```
1. Traverse the left subtree, i.e., call Inorder(left-
subtree)
2. Visit the root.
3. Traverse the right subtree, i.e., call Inorder(right-
subtree)
```

5.3. Postorder Traversal (Left, Right, Root)

The Postorder traversal strategy first traverses the left subtree, then the right subtree, and finally visits the root node.

This approach is useful in mathematical expression trees to obtain the postfix notation (also known as Reverse Polish notation) of an expression. Moreover, this kind of traversal is also used when you need to delete a tree; you delete the children first before you delete the parent node.

Here is the algorithm to implement Postorder traversal:

```
1. Traverse the left subtree, i.e., call Postorder(left-
subtree)
2. Traverse the right subtree, i.e., call
Postorder(right-subtree)
3. Visit the root.
```

It's important to understand that no single traversal is best, and the use of any traversal approach depends entirely on the specific problem at hand.

Through consistent practice and implementation, you can aptly understand the importance and application of these traversal strategies. The ability to choose the correct traversal strategy will undeniably strengthen your problem-solving ability and make you a better programmer in the process.

To maximize your understanding, try implementing these strategies in your favored programming language. Moreover, you can try creating an expression tree and obtain Prefix, Infix, and Postfix notations using Preorder, Inorder, and Postorder traversal, respectively. This exercise will further solidify your grasp on these concepts and their practical application.

Remember, in Computer Science, understanding the underlying theory is as important as its application! Now, equipped with the knowledge of tree traversal, you are one step closer to mastering the mesmerizing world of data structures.

In upcoming sections, we'll explore more intriguing and complex tree algorithms, which will further enhance your comprehension of tree structures.

Chapter 6. Binary Search Trees: Principles and Applications

In the realm of binary trees, binary search trees (BST) stand tall as a specialized variation, providing an efficient method for data storage and retrieval. A BST is a node-based binary tree where each node follows a specific property: the key or value of each node in a BST is greater than the keys of all nodes in its left subtree and less than the keys of all nodes in its right subtree.

6.1. Binary Search Tree Basics

Binary search trees hinge on the concept of ordered data. This inherent property lends them their power, and, at the same time, their potential weaknesses. To get an insight into BSTs, let's delve into the basic node structure. A typical BST node contains three key properties: key or value, a pointer to the left child node, and a pointer to the right child node.

```
|===
| Key | Left | Right

| 50 | 45 | 60
|===
```

The property `Key` is the data or value that the particular node encapsulates. `Left` and `Right` are pointers. They provide a way to navigate through the tree, providing links to the left child and the right child respectively. In the given example, 50 is the root node. 45, being less than 50, becomes the left child whereas 60, being more, becomes the right child.

6.2. BST Operations: Insertion, Deletion, and Search

Binary search trees enable three primary operations: insertion, deletion, and search. These operations work in O(h) time, where h represents the height of the binary search tree.

6.2.1. Insertion in BST

When it comes to insertion, values are compared to the root. If smaller, they move to the left subtree, otherwise to the right. The process continues recursively until the right spot is found.

```
Procedure BSTinsert(tree, node)
If tree is empty, then return node
Else if node.key is less than tree.key
  tree.setLeft(BSTinsert(tree.getLeft, node))
Else
  tree.setRight(BSTinsert(tree.getRight, node))
Return tree
End procedure
```

6.2.2. Deletion in BST

As for deletion, there are three basic scenarios,

1. The node to be removed is a leaf node.

2. The node to be removed has only one child.

3. The node to be removed has two children.

In the first and second cases, we simply remove the node and adjust the corresponding parent pointer. The third case is more involved and requires two steps: find the in-order predecessor or successor node, and replace the node to be deleted with the in-order predecessor or successor.

6.2.3. Searching in BST

Searching is a straightforward operation, akin to insertion. Starting from the root, we move either left or right based on the value compared to the node value, until we hit a dead-end or find the value.

```
Procedure BSTsearch(tree, key)
If tree is null or tree.key is key, then return tree
Else if tree.key is more than key
   Return BSTsearch(tree.getLeft, node)
Else
   Return BSTsearch(tree.getRight, node)
End procedure
```

6.3. The Power of Balance in BSTs

A significant characteristic of binary search trees lies in their height. The performance of a BST is directly proportional to its height. The shorter the BST, the less time it takes to insert, search or delete a node. Therefore, balancing a BST is critical.

Balancing refers to ensuring the left and right subtrees of every node in the BST differ by no more than one in their heights. There are algorithms such as the AVL tree or Red-Black tree which dynamically maintain balance during insertions and deletions.

Although self-balancing binary search trees might seem complex initially, their potential time saving can make them worthwhile especially with enormous datasets in play.

6.4. Applications of BST

Binary search trees have a plethora of applications in computer science. They serve as data structures in programming languages and databases. They enable quick lookup, addition, and removal of items in a dataset. They can also be used to implement dynamic sets and associative arrays.

Binary search trees possess the unique feature of in-order traversal providing a sorted list of numbers, which can be used for sorting algorithms. Additionally, with their ability to maintain data in sorted order, BSTs present an efficient solution to problems involving frequent insertions, deletions and lookups.

In conclusion, BSTs are not only data structures but also a concept that frames our understanding of how complex problems can be tackled with a structured approach. By offering a combination of fast retrieval, insertion, and deletion, Binary Search Trees represent a bedrock of efficient computational problem solving. By mastering them, you gain an essential tool that will come in useful throughout your programming journey.

Chapter 7. Balancing Binary Trees: AVL Trees and Red-Black Trees

Many complex solutions in computer science stem from simple building blocks, albeit arranged and reorganized ingeniously. Take, for instance, the binary tree: a straight-forward data structure that derives its power from dynamism. Once we grasp this structure's elegance, applying it to more advanced variations, like the AVL and Red-Black trees, becomes smoother. Both are types of 'self-balancing' binary search trees, vital for maintaining optimal time complexity. Let's dive deeper into these smart data structures, less used but possessing a depth of beauty of their own.

7.1. Introducing AVL Trees

Named after its inventors, Adelson-Velsky and Landis, the AVL tree offers a balance between read and write operations. An AVL tree is a binary search tree with an added rule: for every node in the tree, the height difference between its left child and right child (known as the 'Balance Factor') is at most 1. This rule ensures that the tree remains balanced and, consequently, searching is efficient.

Essentially, AVL trees aim to avert a situation where you have what's essentially a linked list, disguised as a binary search tree, thus losing the advantage of having a tree structure at all.

7.1.1. Insertion in AVL Trees

Like all binary search trees, insertion in an AVL tree begins by finding the appropriate location. Once inserted, we need to ensure the tree's balance is maintained. If it's not, we perform rotations.

There are four possibilities, depending upon the nature of imbalance detected:

- Left-Left case (LL rotation)

- Left-Right case (LR rotation)

- Right-Right case (RR rotation)

- Right-Left case (RL rotation)

While the code for these rotations could be slightly complex, the underlying concepts are reasonably straightforward.

7.1.2. Deletion in AVL Trees

AVL tree deletion is like binary search tree deletion, but here we again check for imbalance after the operation. If any imbalance is detected, rotations are performed to restored balance.

7.2. Introducing Red-Black Trees

Red-Black tree is another variant of balanced binary search trees, where every node has an extra bit for denoting the color (red or black) of the node. This concept aids in ensuring the tree remains approximately balanced during insertions and deletions.

The rules governing Red-Black trees, offering significant mechanical consequences, are:

- Every node has a color either red or black.

- The root of tree is always black.

- There are no two adjacent red nodes (red node cannot have a red parent or red child).

- Every path from a node (including root) to any of its descendant NULL node has the same number of black nodes.

This structure keeps the tree reasonably well-balanced, enabling operation executions in logarithmic time.

7.2.1. Insertion in Red-Black Trees

The process of inserting a node in a Red-Black tree involves several checks performed during its course. The complexity arises from maintaining the Red-Black tree properties:

1. Insert the node, coloring it red.

2. If it's the root, recolor it black.

3. If its parent is black, relax.

For cases where the parent is red (thus violating Property 3), we perform rotation or recoloring operations to restore properties.

7.2.2. Deletion in Red-Black Trees

Deletion of a node in Red-Black trees can be complicated as it involves several scenarios to consider. The main idea behind deletion is to replace the node with a predecessor, or successor (depending on the scenario), and then adjust the colors and perform rotations to restore properties.

While AVL trees offer faster retrieval times because they're more rigidly balanced, Red-Black trees offer faster insertion and removal times as they're more relaxed, making them suitable for different use cases.

7.3. Conclusion

Both AVL and Red-Black trees have their own niche uses; these self-balancing trees are of paramount importance for maintaining optimized search operations, transforming the way you approach problem-solving in computer science.

This complex yet intriguing exploration is just the beginning of your relationship with data structures, likely to continue evolving with each line of code you write, each problem you solve, and each software you help craft.

Chapter 8. Binary Heap: Implementation and Operations

A Binary Heap is one form of a binary tree. It is a complete binary tree, i.e., it is entirely filled apart from the rightmost elements on the last level. Heaps can be categorized into two types: Min-Heap and Max-Heap.

Min-Heap: In a Min-Heap, for any given node i, its value will be ≤ to its children.

Max-Heap: It's the opposite, where for any given node i, its value will be ≥ to its children.

Let's delve a bit more in-depth on how to implement a Binary Heap and the operations surrounding it.

8.1. Heap Representation

A Binary Heap can be conveniently represented as an array. The root of the tree is the first element `Arr[0]`. For any element of the array `Arr[i]`, its parent will be at `Arr[floor((i-1)/2)]`, its left child at `Arr[(2*i)+1]`, and its right child at `Arr[(2*i)+2]`.

In a Python-esque pseudo-code, the representations would look like this:

```
def parent(i):
    return floor((i-1)/2)

def left_child(i):
```

```
    return 2 * i + 1

def right_child(i):

    return 2 * i + 2
```

8.2. Heap Operations

Here are some principal operations performed on heaps. While we
will discuss them in the context of a Max-Heap, they can be easily
adapted to Min-Heaps.

1. Max-Heapify

2. Build-Max-Heap

3. Heap-Sort

4. Maximum

5. Extract-Max

6. Increase-Key

7. Insert

8.3. Max-Heapify

For an element `Arr[i]` whose left and right children are max-heaps,
but `Arr[i]` itself might not hold the property of not being greater than
its children, Max-Heapify converts the binary tree into a max-heap,
provided the trees rooted at its children are max-heaps.

In Python-esque pseudo code, the `Max-Heapify` function would look
like this:

```
def MaxHeapify(A, i, heap_size):
```

```
        l = left_child(i)
        r = right_child(i)

        if l < heap_size and A[l] > A[i]:
            largest = l
        else:
            largest = i

        if r < heap_size and A[r] > A[largest]:
            largest = r

        if largest != i:
            swap(A[i], A[largest])
            MaxHeapify(A, largest, heap_size)
```

Here, 'swap' simply interchanges the values A[i] and A[largest].

8.4. Build-Max-Heap

To construct a max-heap from any given array or list, we will have to call the MaxHeapify. When starting from the end of the list, as given below, Build-Max-Heap assures that the smaller heaps maintain their structure when the root is heapified.

```
def Build_max_heap(A):

    heap_size = len(A)
    for i in range(heap_size, -1, -1):
        MaxHeapify(A, i, heap_size)
```

8.5. Heap-Sort

The heap sort algorithm can be viewed as an improved selection sort. As selection sort finds the minimum element and puts it at the front, heap sort likewise finds the maximum element, places it at the end, reduces the heap size by one, and heapifies the root for the reduced heap. This process is iterated until all elements are sorted.

```python
def Heapsort(A):

    Build_max_heap(A)
    heap_size = len(A)

    for i in range(heap_size - 1, 0, -1):
        swap(A[0], A[i])
        heap_size = heap_size - 1
        MaxHeapify(A, 0, heap_size)
```

8.6. Maximum

In a max heap, the maximum key will always be at the root (i.e., Arr[0]).

```python
def maximum(A):
    return A[0]
```

8.7. Extract-Max

To retrieve and remove the maximum element from a max heap, we move the last element to the root and then reduce the size of the heap by one. To preserve the max heap structure, we heapify the root.

```
def extract_max(A):

    if len(A) < 1:
        return "Heap underflow"
    max = A[0]
    A[0] = A[len(A) - 1]
    MaxHeapify(A, 0, len(A) - 1)

    return max
```

8.8. Increase-Key

The key of any element can be increased using this function. If the updated key is larger, then the element moves up until its key $\geq$ children.

```
def Increase_key(A,i,key):

    if key<A[i]:
        return "New key is smaller than current key"
    A[i]=key
    while i>0 and A[parent(i)]<A[i] :
        swap(A[i],A[parent(i)])
        i = parent(i)
```

8.9. Insert

The Insert operation is performed by adding the element at the bottom-most rightmost position and then pushing it upwards till it is in its correct position.

```
def Insert(A,key):
```

```
A.append(-1)
Increase_key(A,len(A)-1,key)
```

In conclusion, these operations on binary heaps form the basis for various algorithms and data structures like priority queues, graph algorithms, etc. These concepts, once understood and mastered, will increase your proficiency and flexibility when it comes to dealing with tree or heap-based data structure problems. They are an essential part of the programming world and offer a unique and efficient approach to organizing and accessing data.

Chapter 9. Comparison on Performance: From Binary Trees to B-Trees

Performance comparison of data structures is a crucial task as it provides deeper insights into the advantages and disadvantages of using each one under different situations. In this chapter, we will be focusing on the comparison between Binary Trees and B-Trees, two widely used tree structures.

9.1. Understanding Binary Trees and Their Performance Characteristics

Before delving into the comparative analysis, let's first get an understanding of binary trees and their performance characteristics. A binary tree is a tree-like data structure where each node has at most two children. It has a key part that holds the data, and two pointers for the left and the right child nodes.

The performance characteristics of binary trees are predominantly determined by their height, which is the maximum number of edges from the root to the leaf. The lesser the height, the better the performance. The time complexity for search, insert, and delete operations in a binary tree is O(h), where h is the height of the tree.

9.2. Understanding B-Trees and Their Performance Characteristics

Now turning towards B-Trees, they are an extension of binary trees that allows for more than two child nodes. A B-Tree of order m has a maximum of m children.

Unlike binary trees, B-trees are balanced. The operations insert, delete, and search take O(log n) time, where n is the number of keys. This makes B-trees an excellent choice for large data sets stored in secondary storage such as disks.

9.3. Comparing Binary Trees and B-Trees on Basis of Operations

When performing basic operations such as insertion, deletion, and search, B-Trees generally have the edge due to their logarithmic time complexity.

Insertion in a binary tree involves finding the correct place for insertion, which takes O(h) time. On the contrary, despite being a more elaborate process, insertion in a B-Tree takes O(log n) time, making it more efficient for larger data sets.

Deletion, like insertion, in a binary tree consumes O(h) time since deletion involves searching the node and then restructuring the tree. Whereas in a B-Tree, despite the intrinsic complexity to maintain the properties of a B-Tree after deletion, it still performs better by taking O(log n) time due to its balanced nature.

Lastly, when it comes to searching, both binary trees and B-Trees show a difference in time complexity. Again, B-Trees outperform with an average and worst-case complexity of O(log n), while a binary search tree (best version of binary trees for searching) has an average complexity of O(log n) but a worse case complexity of O(n) when the tree becomes skewed.

9.4. Comparing Binary Trees and B-Trees on Basis of Space Usage

Comparing on the basis of space usage, both trees have their merits and demerits. Binary trees use less space as each node stores only one key and pointers to two children. However, in the case of a binary search tree, they can become skewed, resulting in poor space utilization.

On the other hand, B-Trees use more space as they store multiple keys per node and have pointers to many children. However, thanks to their balanced nature and branching factor, they tend to utilize space more efficiently when dealing with large data sets, hence reducing the height of the tree and improving speed.

To summarize, B-Trees tend to be more efficient than binary trees when dealing with larger data sets, especially those that don't fit into main memory. However, binary trees are simpler and might be more suitable for smaller data sets or when simplicity is prioritized over efficiency.

This chapter aims to provide an in-depth understanding of the performance intricacies between binary trees and B-trees. It was our attempt to compare and contrast these two tree-based data structures that find numerous applications in handling data in a structured and accessible format. Understanding these details will provide a solid foundation for making an informed decision about which data structure to use based on your specific requirements in terms of speed, space, and complexity.

Chapter 10. Real-World Applications of Binary Trees

Binary trees, a key non-linear data structure, hold a crucial space in computer science with diverse and meaningful real-world applications. Their unique structure simplifies complicated processes, hence enabling a more effective and streamlined computational experience. Some key areas where binary trees are applied significantly include databases, routers, computer graphics, and complex algorithms, which are explained in detail throughout this chapter.

10.1. Utilization in Database Systems

Database systems extensively use binary trees. Particularly, B-Trees, a variant of binary trees, are omnipresent in the data storage structures of popular database systems.

1. **Indexing**: Binary Trees serve as the backbone of database indexing. Implementations such as B-trees and B+ trees are immensely popular. Index records in these trees correspond to a certain key and pointer pairs, enabling efficient data retrieval. The tree structure allows the database system to minify disk reads, drastically boosting performance.

2. **Query Optimization**: Database systems craft their query plans rooted in the structures of binary trees. These so-called Query Trees aid in effectively evaluating SQL queries, hence offering optimal data retrieval paths.

10.2. Application in Routers

The underlying science in IP routing is, at heart, an exercise in using binary trees. Digital Trees (or "tries")—a type of binary tree—are at the core of the longest prefix matching algorithm used for IP routing.

1. **Longest Prefix Matching**: Binary tries enable routers to find the network which has the longest prefix matching with the incoming IP address. The binary tree efficiently stores the routing table, where each node represents a possible network address and the edges represent direct connections.

10.3. Role in Computer Graphics

Binary space partitioning trees (BSP trees) are a particular type of binary tree used extensively in computer graphics, video games and CAD (Computer Aided Design). They elegantly solve visibility problems and help deal with complex spatial information.

1. **Image Rendering**: BSP trees are employed in image rendering to determine which objects are visible and which are hidden. They enable the visibility of an image from a particular viewpoint to be determined discarding occluded parts efficiently.

2. **Collision Detection**: Binary trees expedite the process of collision detection in video games, by partitioning space into manageable subsections, significantly reducing mathematical computations.

10.4. Binary Trees in Advanced Algorithms

Binary trees are fundamentally important in several complex algorithms applied across various fields of computer science.

1. **Compression Algorithms**: Huffman Trees—a special type of binary tree—are extensively used in data compression algorithms. The Huffman coding algorithm represents data using varying lengths of binary codes with frequently occurring characters utilizing shorter codes, consequently optimizing data storage or transmission.

2. **Convex Hull**: The QuickHull algorithm used for solving the Convex Hull problem utilizes binary trees for its implementation. The algorithm works by recursively dividing the problem into subproblems (similar to divide and conquer), where each node of the tree can represent a separate subproblem.

Binary trees, with their distinctive characteristics, have naturally found their way into diverse applications far beyond these mentioned. Their widespread usage can be attributed to their ability to provide a firm structure, which opens avenues for optimization and efficiency. It's the innate power of binary trees that truly underpins the realm of advanced computer science—offering not only the optimum frameworks to solve complex problems but also encouraging us to consider and visualize intricate systems from an entirely new perspective.

Chapter 11. Conclusion: The Future of Tree-based Structures

Binary trees and tree-based structures have become the bedrock of computer programming. Their hierarchical structure is a cornerstone in organizing data and information efficiently. However, our journey does not conclude here - the future holds an even greater promise for these powerful tools.

As quantum computing bounds towards us and the rise of artificial intelligence (AI) revolutionizes the tech world, the role of trees in information science stands to take a significant leap forward. The form and function of tree data structures will undoubtedly evolve to meet these thrilling new challenges.

11.1. Quantum Computing and Trees

Quantum computing is on the horizon, and it has the potential to revolutionize computing in ways we cannot fully fathom. Quantum algorithms could drastically cut down computation times for many problems that classical computers struggle to solve. This challenges us to reimagine our data structures, to envision how they might operate in this strange new world.

Quantum trees could aid selection and search processes, forming the basis of new, efficient quantum algorithms. Such trees could store and manage quantum bits (qubits) instead of the classical bits stored in our current trees. They could define hierarchical relationships between qubits, creating a structured ecosystem to manipulate these fragile and volatile entities.

11.2. AI and Trees

Artificial Intelligence and Machine Learning are no longer the future - they are the present. The tree-based structure, amidst this AI evolution, offers an unprecedented advantage. Decision Trees are one of the prime examples of how tree structures aren't relegated to the background but stand at the forefront of AI development.

The Decision Tree algorithm partitions the sample space sequentially, leveraging tree structures to navigate through potential solutions. The role of Binary Trees and other tree-based structures might expand and diversify, as AI advances requiring more sophisticated decision-making models.

11.3. Advanced Data Structures

As we tackle more complex computational problems, we may need to adapt our understanding of trees accordingly. Future computer scientists might use trees as building blocks to design yet unimagined data structures. These advanced designs could balance efficiency and flexibility far better than current structures, especially as new types of data emerge.

11.4. Automobile and Traffic Systems

Looking ahead, tree-based structures might take a new turn by expanding their realm into managing automobile and traffic systems. With the advent of self-driving cars, these could become a necessity. Tree-structures could provide a way for the AI in self-perpetuating cars to make decisions.

The potential use case may include employing Weighted Binary trees, designed with weights assigned to each node to calculate quickest routes. The weights might denote traffic congestion, and the AI could dynamically update the tree as traffic conditions change.

11.5. Cybersecurity

With increasing data breaches, cybersecurity has commandeered global attention. Binary Trees could prove instrumental in enhancing cybersecurity. It might play a vital role in building encrypted systems. Binary Search Trees can execute operations like search, insertion, and deletion in logarithmic time, which is incredibly useful for password verification and managing user databases.

11.6. Space Exploration

Data structures might also expand towards controlling space exploration missions. Everything from establishing communication with rovers on Mars to launching measures for protecting our planet from asteroids could potentially leverage tree-based systems.

Binary Trees could be utilized in programming automated spacecraft, achieving better navigational control for interplanetary missions. Advanced tree structures might pave the way for more automated and efficient extraterrestrial explorations.

In conclusion, binary trees, as humble as they may look, are one of the pillars of Computer Science. They continue to form the backbone of modern database and file systems. As the future unfolds, tree structures are well-poised to become even more vital in our increasingly digital and connected world — from improving AI algorithms to managing future quantum computers.

Your understanding of binary trees is not just a useful skill in the present, but an investment for the future. This knowledge takes you a step ahead on the path of computer science - a field that is bound to keep evolving and surprising us with its limitless potential.

www.ingramcontent.com/pod-product-compliance
Lightning Source LLC
Chambersburg PA
CBHW071012260726
48661CB00007B/2922